DATE DUE

919.8   BC#34880000024997 $25.36
FOS   Foster, Leila Merrell
         Antarctica

Morrill E.S.
Chicago Public Schools
1431 North Leamington Avenue
Chicago, IL 60651

CONTINENTS

Antarctica

Leila Merrell Foster

Heinemann Library
Chicago, Illinois

Designed by Joanna Hinton-Malivoire and Q2A Creative
Printed in China by South China Printing Company

10 09 08 07 06
10 9 8 7 6 5 4 3 2 1

New edition ISBN: 1-4034-8540-2 (hardcover)
                  1-4034-8548-8 (paperback)

The Library of Congress has cataloged the first edition as follows:
Foster, Leila Merrell.
          Antarctica / Leila Merrell Foster.
                   p. cm. – (Continents)
          Includes bibliographical references and index.
          ISBN 1-57572-447-2
          1. Antarctica – Juvenile literature. 2. Ecology – Antarctica – Juvenile literature. [1. Antarctica.] I. Title. II.
Continents (Chicago, Ill.)
G863 .F67 2001
919.8'9—dc21   00-011465

Acknowledgments
The publishers are grateful to the following for permission to reproduce copyright material: Tony Stone/Ben Osborne p. 5; Earth Scenes/David C. Fritts p. 6; Tony Stone/Kim Heacox p. 7; Peter Arnold/Gordon Wiltsie pp. 8, 13; Getty Images/ National Geographic/ Ralph Lee Hopkins p.10; Tony Stone/Kim Westerskov pp. 11, 17, 28; Photo Edit/ Anna Zuckermann p. 15; Photo Edit/Jack S. Grove p. 16; Bruce Coleman/Fritz Polking, Inc. p. 20; Animals Animals/ Johnny Johnson p. 21; Earth Scenes/Stefano Nicolini p. 22; Earth Scenes/Patti Murray p. 23; Corbis/Bettmann Archive p. 24; The Granger Collection p. 25; Peter Arnold/Bruno P. Zehnder p. 27; Earth Scenes/B. Herrod p. 29.

Cover photograph of Antarctica, reproduced with permission of Science Photo Library/ Tom Van Sant, Geosphere Project/ Planetary Visions.

The publishers would like to thank Kathy Peltan, Keith Lye, and Nancy Harris for their assistance in the preparation of this book.

Every effort has been made to contact copyright holders of any material reproduced in this book. Any omissions will be rectified in subsequent printings if notice is given to the publisher.

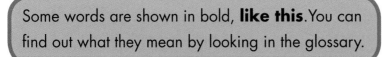

Some words are shown in bold, **like this**. You can find out what they mean by looking in the glossary.

Contents

Where Is Antarctica?

A continent is a very large area of land. There are seven continents in the world. Antarctica is farther south than any other continent. This means it is very cold there.

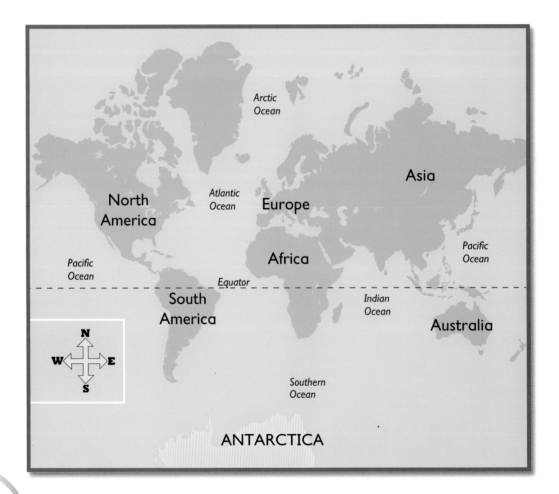

ANTARCTICA

The world's lowest temperature was recorded in Antarctica. It was -128.6 °F (-89.2 °C).

▲ Snow-covered mountains are found in Antarctica.

The **South Pole** is at the center of Antarctica. Close to the South Pole, the sun sets only once a year. It is dark for six months in winter and light for six months in summer.

Ice Sheet

It is so cold in Antarctica that the snow does not **melt**. The snow builds up into layers of ice. The ice covers nearly all of the land. This is known as the Antarctic **ice sheet**.

▲ *These mountains are buried under ice.*

The Antarctic ice sheet holds over two-thirds of all the fresh water in the world.

▲ This **iceberg** is close to the ice sheet.

The Antarctic ice sheet is very thick. If it ever melted, the level of all of the seas in the world would rise by almost 200 feet (60 meters). All the towns and cities along the coasts would disappear underwater.

South Pole

On the map there is a circle called the Antarctic Circle. It is an imaginary line that goes around the continent of Antarctica. Almost all of Antarctica is inside the Antarctic Circle.

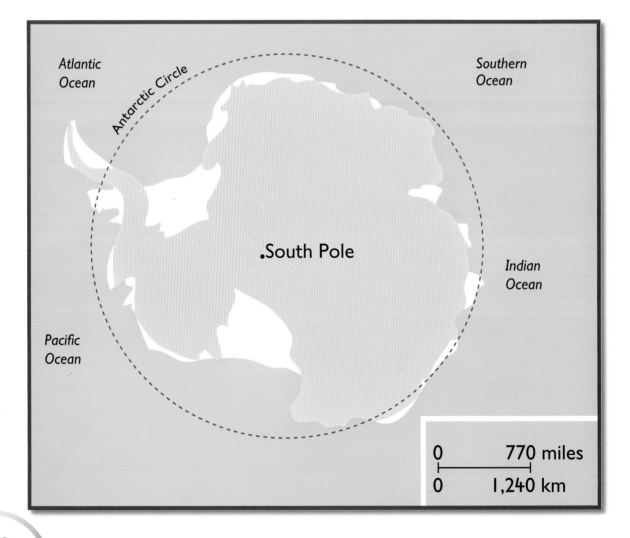

Atlantic Ocean

Antarctic Circle

Southern Ocean

.South Pole

Indian Ocean

Pacific Ocean

| 0 | 770 miles |
| 0 | 1,240 km |

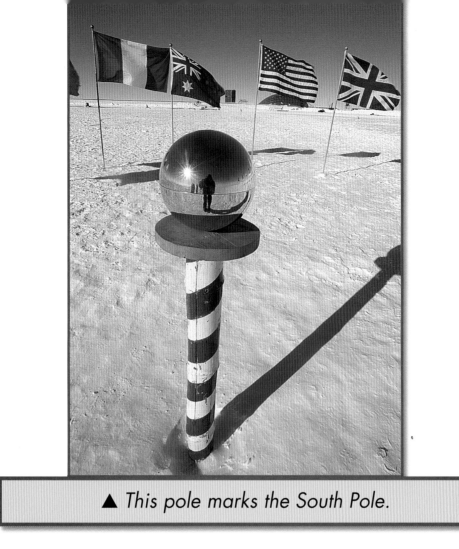

▲ *This pole marks the South Pole.*

The **North Pole** and the **South Pole** are the farthest places from the **Equator**. The Equator is an imaginary line around the center of Earth. The North Pole is in the Arctic. The South Pole is in Antarctica.

Weather

In summer some of the ice at the edge of the **ice sheet melts**. In winter the sea at the edge freezes again. This frozen seawater is called pack ice.

▲ *Penguins live on the ice.*

Antarctica is the coldest and windiest place on Earth.

▲ *There is icy desert in central Antarctica.*

In the center of Antarctica, there is an icy **desert**. Very little snow falls there, but sometimes there are **blizzards** that last for days. Human skin can freeze in 60 seconds. Even in summer, the temperature hardly ever gets above the **freezing point**.

Mountains

The Transantarctic Mountains run right across Antarctica. They divide the continent into two areas. The areas are called Greater Antarctica and Lesser Antarctica. Greater Antarctica is a huge **dome** of ice.

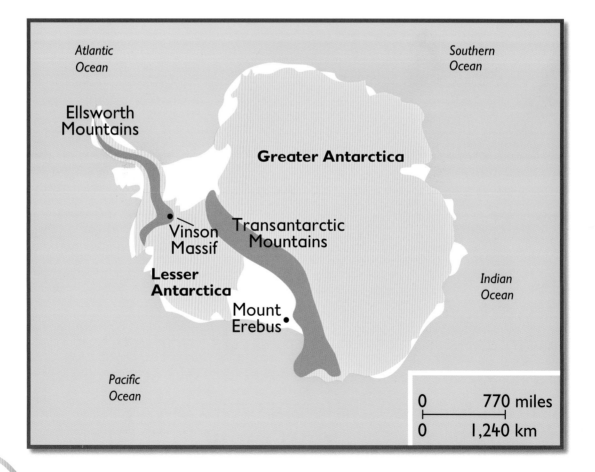

The Vinson Massif is the highest point in Antarctica.

▲ *The Vinson Massif is in the Ellsworth Mountains.*

The Vinson **Massif** is in the Ellsworth Mountains, in western Antarctica. Mount Erebus is an **active volcano**. Mount Erebus often **erupts**. This means it throws out rocks.

Ice

Huge shelves of ice hang over the sea around the edges of Antarctica. They are called ice shelves. Some of these ice shelves are huge. When chunks of ice break away in the summer months, they form **icebergs**.

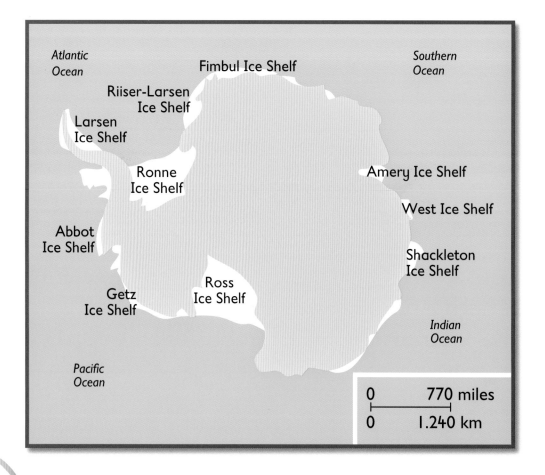

Atlantic Ocean

Fimbul Ice Shelf

Southern Ocean

Riiser-Larsen Ice Shelf

Larsen Ice Shelf

Ronne Ice Shelf

Amery Ice Shelf

West Ice Shelf

Abbot Ice Shelf

Shackleton Ice Shelf

Getz Ice Shelf

Ross Ice Shelf

Indian Ocean

Pacific Ocean

0	770 miles
0	1.240 km

Most of an iceberg is hidden below the water.

▲ *Icebergs drift in the ocean.*

Strong **currents** carry the icebergs out to sea. Icebergs are very dangerous for ships. This is because they are much larger than they seem. It can take many years for icebergs to **melt** and crack apart.

Glaciers

The continent of Antarctica is shaped like a **dome**. Ice is formed in the high center of Antarctica. Then, the ice slowly slides down the slopes of the dome to the edge of Antarctica. These slow rivers of ice are called **glaciers**.

▲ *This glacier is on the Antarctic coast.*

The Lambert Glacier is the world's largest glacier.

▲ *This ice cliff is at the edge of a glacier.*

The ice at the bottom of the glacier gets crushed by the ice above. Then, the whole glacier slowly slides forward. Glaciers often look like huge cliffs of ice.

Oceans and Seas

Antarctica is surrounded by the icy cold Southern Ocean. There are also smaller seas closer to the land. The Southern Ocean stops the warmer water in other oceans from reaching the ice, so the ice does not **melt**.

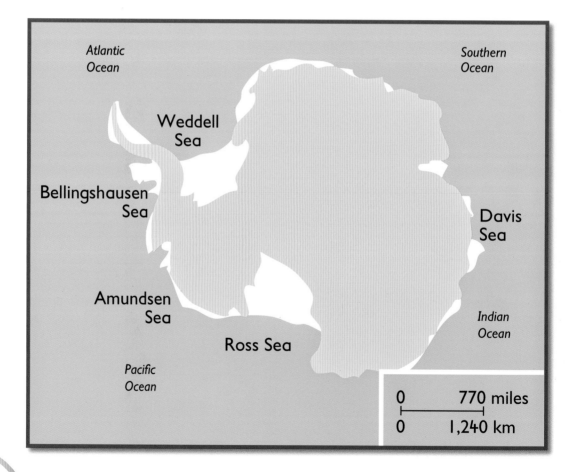

Atlantic Ocean

Southern Ocean

Weddell Sea

Bellingshausen Sea

Davis Sea

Amundsen Sea

Indian Ocean

Ross Sea

Pacific Ocean

| 0 | 770 miles |
| 0 | 1,240 km |

▲ *This shows stormy weather in the Southern Ocean.*

The Southern Ocean has strong **currents**. It has strong winds and huge waves. Most ships that go to Antarctica leave from the tip of South America. The journey takes three days in calm weather. When it is stormy, it can take weeks.

Animals

Most birds that visit Antarctica fly north for the winter. But penguins stay in Antarctica all year round. Penguins have a thick layer of fat as well as soft feathers to keep them warm. They are excellent swimmers. They catch fish from the sea.

▲ *Emperor penguins live in Antarctica.*

▲ *An elephant seal's nose looks like an elephant's trunk.*

There are also seals and whales. The seals spend most of their time hunting for fish in the icy seas. People used to hunt the whales and seals that live in Antarctica. Now, there are laws to protect them.

Plants

Lichen is the most common plant in Antarctica. It grows on rocks. It needs very little water to survive. Some types of moss also grow in Antarctica. Moss and lichen grow very slowly.

Some of the moss and lichen plants in Antarctica are more than 1,000 years old.

▲ *Lichen grows on rocks.*

Tussock grass is the only grass that grows in Antarctica.

▲ *Tussock grass grows in northern Antarctica.*

No trees grow in Antarctica. Only two types of flowering plant have ever been found there. Tussock grass is a type of grass that is found in the warmest parts of the continent. It has very strong roots to stop it from being blown away.

Explorers

Early explorers sailed to Antarctica in wooden ships. But the sea ice trapped their boats. A British explorer named Ernest Shackleton escaped from his ship in a lifeboat. Some of his crew drifted for five months before they reached land.

▲ *Ernest Shakleton's ship was trapped in ice.*

▲ *Roald Amundsen was a Norwegian explorer.*

Roald Amundsen was the first person to reach the **South Pole**. He reached it in 1911. A British explorer, Robert Scott, reached the South Pole in 1912. He used ponies to pull his sled. Sadly, he died on the journey home.

Research Stations

Antarctica is the only continent with no countries. Many countries send scientists there to work in **research stations**. These scientists do **experiments** on the ice. The map shows some of the main stations in Antarctica and the countries they belong to.

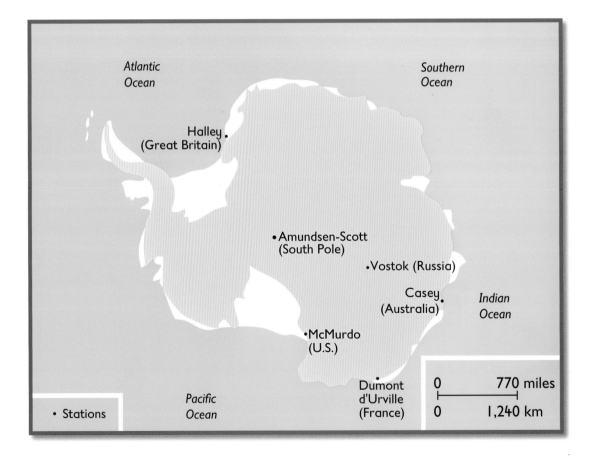

Atlantic Ocean

Southern Ocean

Halley (Great Britain)

• Amundsen-Scott (South Pole)

• Vostok (Russia)

Casey (Australia)

Indian Ocean

• McMurdo (U.S.)

Dumont d'Urville (France)

Pacific Ocean

• Stations

0 — 770 miles
0 — 1,240 km

▲ *This is the McMurdo Research Station in Antarctica.*

In 1959 twelve countries agreed to keep Antarctica free for peaceful research. **Mining** is not allowed there. During the summer, small groups of tourists visit Antarctica. They must not leave any garbage behind.

Science

Scientists study the weather in Antarctica. This helps them understand the weather all over the world. They measure how much ice **melts** in summer. They have discovered that more ice melts each year. This means the world's weather is getting warmer.

▲ *Scientists use a weather balloon to test gases in the air.*

▲ Scientists set up equipment on the ice.

Some scientists drill into the ice to find out what the weather was like hundreds of years ago. Other scientists in Antarctica study animals and plants or use powerful telescopes to look at the stars.

Fast Facts

Antarctica's highest mountains

Name of mountain	Height in feet	Height in meters
Vinson Massif	16,077	4,897
Mount Tyree	15,918	4,852
Mount Kirkpatrick	14,855	4,528
Mount Markham	14,271	4,350
Mount Erebus	12,448	3,794

Antarctica's record breakers

The coldest temperature ever recorded was at Vostock **Research Station**, Antarctica, in 1983. It was –128.6 °F (–89.2 °C).

No rain falls on the land in Antarctica. It only rains around the edge of the coast.

Winds in the Southern Ocean around Antarctica can reach speeds of about 185 miles (300 kilometers) per hour.

At its thickest point, the ice covering Antarctica is about 16 feet (almost 5 kilometers) deep. Most of the ice in Antarctica is about 6.5 feet (2 kilometers) deep.

Antarctica contains two-thirds of the world's fresh water in the form of ice.

The biggest **iceberg** ever seen was larger than Maryland. It covered about 11,600 square miles (about 30,000 square kilometers).

The Lambert **Glacier** is more than 250 miles (400 kilometers) long and 25 miles (80 kilometers) wide at the base.

Scientists have found fossils in Antarctica. This means that the continent was once warm, and that trees and other plants once lived there.

Glossary

active volcano hole in the earth from which hot, melted rock is thrown out

blizzard snowstorm in which surface snow is picked up by strong winds

current movement of water

desert area with very little rain

dome rounded shape, like half a ball

Equator imaginary circle around the exact middle of Earth

erupt to throw out rocks and hot ash

experiment test to show or prove something

freezing point 32 °F (0 °C), the temperature at which water freezes

glacier very large mass of slow-moving ice and snow

iceberg large piece of ice that floats in the ocean

ice sheet very thick layer of ice that covers a large area of land

massif mountainous area with lots of peaks

melt become liquid through heat

mining digging up things from under Earth's surface

North Pole most northern spot on Earth

research station place where scientists work to find out new things

South Pole most southern spot on Earth

More Books to Read

Royston, Angela. *Oceans*. Chicago: Heinemann Library, 2005.

Spilsbury, Louise and Richard. *Watching Penguins in Antarctica*. Chicago: Heinemann Library, 2006.

Index